Draw
Children

GW00391347

ROY SPENCER

Series editors: David and Brenda Herbert

A & C Black • London

First published 1981
New style of paperback binding 1996
by A&C Black Publishers
37 Soho Square
London W1D 3QZ

Reprinted 2002

ISBN 0-7136-6489-4

Printed in Hong Kong by Wing King Tong

Cover photograph by Zul Mukhida

Contents

Making
a start

Learning to draw is largely a matter of practice and observation —
so draw as much and as often as you can, and use your eyes all the
time.

Look around you — at chairs, tables, plants, people, pets,
buildings, your hand holding this book. Everything is worth
drawing. The time spent on a drawing is not important. It is the
intensity and purpose with which it is done that matters.

Carry a sketchbook with you whenever possible, and don't be shy
of using it in public, either for quick notes to be used later or for a
finished drawing.

To do an interesting drawing, you must enjoy it. Even if you start on something that doesn't particularly interest you, you will probably find that the act of drawing it — and looking at it in a new way — creates its own excitement. The less you think about how you are drawing and the more you think about what you are drawing, the better your drawing will be.

Be as bold as you dare. It's your piece of paper and you can do what you like with it. Experiment with the biggest piece of paper and the boldest, softest piece of chalk or crayon you can find, filling the paper with lines — scribbles, lettering, anything — to get a feeling of freedom. Even if you think you have a gift for tiny delicate line drawings with a fine pen or pencil, this is worth trying. It will give you an idea of how vivid a drawing can be.

Be self-critical. The aim is to get the drawing right; so alter it to make it so using an eraser as little as possible. This does not mean retracing lines more heavily. A drawing is the sum total of all your efforts to get it right. Neatness does not make a good drawing.

It is preferable to draw in black and white, and to use colour when it says something about the subject which you cannot say in black and white alone.

You can learn a certain amount from copying other people's drawings. But you will learn more from a drawing done from direct observation of the subject or even out of your head, however stiff and unsatisfactory the results may seem at first.

A lot can be learned by practice and from books, but a teacher can be a great help. If you get the chance, don't hesitate to join a class — even one evening a week can do a lot of good.

What to draw with

Pencils are graded according to hardness, from 6H (the hardest) through 5H, 4H, 3H, 2H to H; then HB; then B, through 1B, 2B, 3B, 4B, 5B up to 6B (the softest). For most purposes, a soft pencil (HB or softer) is best. If you keep it sharp, it will draw as fine a line as a hard pencil but with less pressure, which makes it easier to control.

Charcoal, which is very soft, is by nature useful for bold drawing, but with skill you can achieve great subtlety with it. Charcoal pencils, such as the Royal Sovereign are also very useful.

Wax crayons (also soft) are not easily smudged or erased. You can scrape a line away from a drawing on good quality paper, or partly scrape a drawing to get special effects.

Conté crayons, wood-cased or in solid sticks, are available in various degrees of hardness, and in three colours — black, red and white. The cased crayons are easy to sharpen, but the solid sticks are more fun — you can use the side of the stick for large areas of tone. Conté is harder than charcoal, but it is also easy to smudge. The black is very intense.

Pastels are very soft and available in a wide range of colours. Nevertheless many of the best drawings have been done with a very limited number of colours.

Pens vary as much as pencils or crayons. The Gillott 659 is a very popular crowquill pen. Ink has a quality of its own, but of course it cannot be erased. Mapping pens are only suitable for delicate detail and minute cross-hatching.

Special artists' pens, such as the Gillott 303 or Gillott 404 allow you a more varied line, according to the angle at which you hold them and the pressure you use.

Reed, bamboo and quill pens are good for bold lines. You can make the nib end narrower or wider with the help of a sharp knife or razor blade. This kind of pen has to be dipped frequently into the ink.

Fountain pens are convenient for sketching, provided they make a fairly even line in any direction. Rapidograph and Rotring pens are not generally desirable. They are really for mechanical drawing.

Inks vary according to the manufacturer. Waterproof Indian ink is generally the most useful. If it is too thick and clogs the pen, water it down with distilled water or boiled water out of the kettle. It is very necessary to use a waterproof ink if you intend to use it as a wash.

Ball point pens make a drawing look a bit mechanical, but they are cheap and fool-proof and useful for quick notes and scribbles.

Fibre pens are only slightly better, and their points tend to wear down quickly.

Felt pens are useful for quick notes and sketches, but are not good for more elaborate and finished drawings.

Brushes are most versatile drawing instruments and therefore very difficult to use. The Chinese and Japanese until recently have never used anything else, even for writing. The biggest sable brush has a fine point, and the smallest brush laid on its side provides a line broader than the broadest nib. Sables are very expensive but you can find cheaper brushes which are less springy and good to use.

A wash of watercolour or ink may be used to extend a pen or pencil drawing. It should not be used for effect but to say something about the subject, such as the pattern of colour or the light and shade.

What to draw on

'What to draw on' and 'what to draw with' depend on each other. A pencil drawing needs fairly smooth paper with a good 'bite'—the smaller the drawing, the smoother the paper. A pen drawing needs a hard, white paper; and a pen-and-wash drawing a softer, more absorbent paper. Try out as many different surfaces as possible.

Ordinary, inexpensive paper is often as good as anything else: for example, brown and buff wrapping paper (Kraft paper) and lining for wallpaper have surfaces which are particularly suitable for charcoal and soft crayons. Some writing and duplicating papers are best for pen drawings. But there are many papers and brands made specially for the artist.

Bristol board is a smooth, hard white board designed for fine pen work.

Ledger Bond paper ('cartridge' in the UK), the most usual drawing paper, is available in a variety of surfaces — smooth, 'not surface' (semi-rough), rough.

Watercolour papers also come in various grades of smoothness. They are thick, high-quality papers, expensive but pleasant to use.

Ingres paper is mainly for pastel drawings. It has a soft, furry surface and is made in many light colours — grey, pink, blue, buff, etc.

Sketchbooks made up from nearly all these papers, are available. Choose one with thin, smooth paper to begin with. Thin paper means more pages, and a smooth surface is best to record detail.

Lay-out pads make useful sketchbooks. Although their covers are not stiff, you can easily insert a stiff piece of card to act as firm backing to your drawing. The paper is semi-transparent, but this can be useful — almost as tracing paper — if you want to make a new, different version of your last drawing.

An improvised sketchbook can be just as good as a bought one — or better. Find two pieces of thick card, sandwich a stack of paper, which may be of different kinds, between them and clip together at either end.

Pen on very smooth cartridge.

Pen on ordinary cartridge.

Charcoal on Ingres paper.

Perspective: general

You can be an artist without knowing anything about perspective. Five hundred years ago, when some of the great masterpieces of all time were painted, the word did not even exist. But most beginners want to know something about it in order to make their drawings appear three-dimensional rather than flat, so here is a short guide.

The futher away an object is, the smaller it looks.

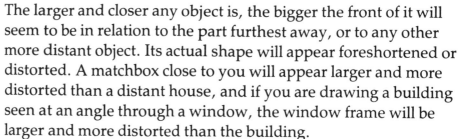

All parallel horizontal lines that are directly opposite you, at right-angles to your line of vision, remain parallel.

All horizontal lines that are in fact parallel but go away from you will appear to converge at eye-level at the same vanishing point on the horizon. Lines that are above your eye-level will seem to run downwards towards the vanishing point; lines that are below your eye-level will run upwards. You can check the angles of these lines against a pencil held horizontally at eye-level.

The larger and closer any object is, the bigger the front of it will seem to be in relation to the part furthest away, or to any other more distant object. Its actual shape will appear foreshortened or distorted. A matchbox close to you will appear larger and more distorted than a distant house, and if you are drawing a building seen at an angle through a window, the window frame will be larger and more distorted than the building.

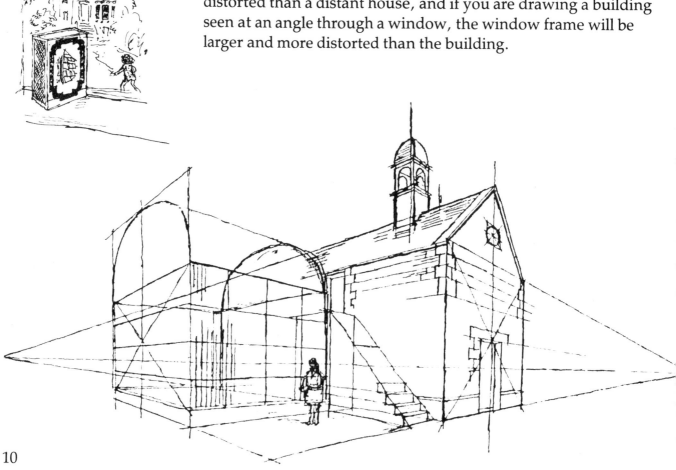

If the side of an object is facing you, one vanishing point is enough; but if the corner is facing you, two vanishing points will be needed.

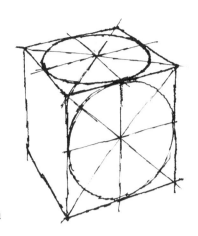

Diagonal lines drawn between the opposite angles of a square or rectangle will meet at a point which is half-way along its length or breadth. This remains true when the square or rectangle is foreshortened. You may find it helpful to remember this when you are drawing surfaces with equal divisions — for example, a tiled floor or the divisions between window panes — or deciding where to place the point of a roof or the position of windows on a facade.

When drawing a circular shape, the following is useful: a square drawn round a circle will touch the circle at the centre point of each of its sides. A foreshortened circle will turn into an elipse, but will still touch the centre points of each side of a similarly foreshortened square. However distorted the square, the circle will remain a true elipse but will seem to tilt as the square moves to left or right of the vanishing point. The same is true of half circles.

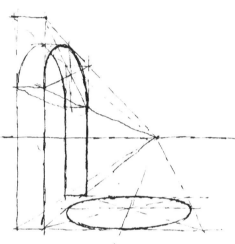

You may tend to exaggerate the apparent depth of top surfaces because you know they are square or rectangular and want to show this in your drawing.

You can check the correct apparent depth of any receding plane by using a pencil or ruler held at eye-level and measuring the proportions on it with your thumb. If you use a ruler you can actually read off the various proportions.

Check the position of parts of a drawing against a horizontal or vertical. We are all agreed as to what they are.

The same applies when you are drawing figures. If, for example, you try to draw a foreshortened forehead or arm you will tend to draw it the shape you know it to be rather than the shape it appears to be from your viewpoint. Again, measuring one proportion against another will help you to make your drawing look right.

Although perspective comes close to what we see, it is nevertheless a system of drawing and only makes sense when the view is seen within limited angles of vision. By extending the diagonal to construct a square on the pavement nearer to you (as in the diagram on the right) a square is produced of absurd

proportions. If you were to extend the drawing sideways the same unreal shapes would occur.

The eye-level need not of course be that of figures in the scene. You may be sitting down or at a higher level. If you are seated, the nearer the standing figures the higher their heads will be. Try some perspective studies with different eye-levels and draw from a subject to see how these principles are borne out in reality.

Perspective: figures

All objects on your eye-level, whether they are close to you or far away, and (if they are people) whether standing or sitting, must always be on the same horizontal in your picture.

Make perspective studies from real life scenes. Draw a line across your paper to represent your eye level. Then (without worrying about the quality of your drawing) plot the positions of the heads and feet of the people in the scene in front of you. Discover the point at which parallel horizontal lines converge. The diagrammatic sketches here show the process I went through to produce the drawing on the right.

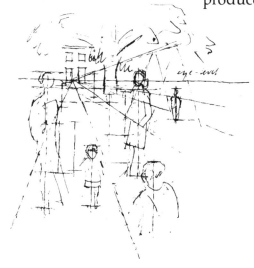

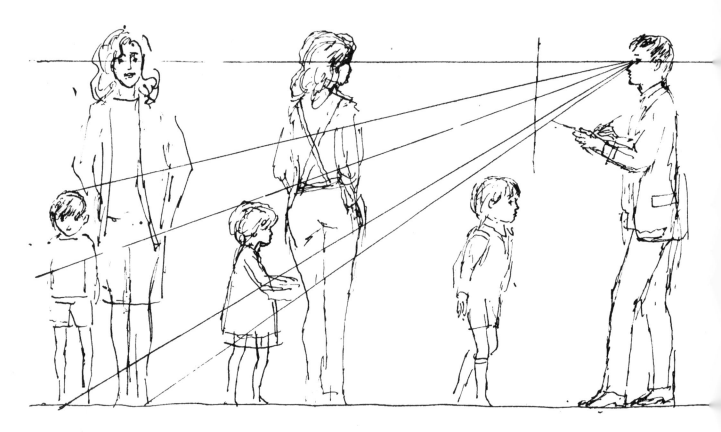

Fore-shortening

When drawing a child's portrait, sit only a few feet from your subject in order to see his features as clearly as possible. This will mean that the lower part of the figure is very foreshortened. Fixing some points by measuring against your pencil can help you, especially, to draw the pattern of the shapes. Foreshortening is particularly troublesome because the perspective becomes steeper and steeper, and the distortion can suggest a disproportioned figure. In the drawings here the chair is essential, in order to explain the geometry of the boy's legs.

Masses and planes

Many drawing problems disappear as soon as you realize that a picture is an *interpretation* of what you see, not an *imitation* of it. The first essential is to represent or imply solid form and space. Don't copy the tone of your subject; try to understand its solid shape as you would that of a cube, and use tone to make the forms you have observed.

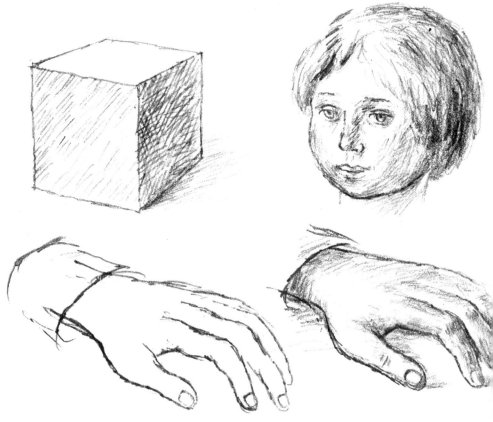

The first drawing here is a ring on the paper, drawn without any suggestion that it represents a solid. In the second, the line moves round as if it were enclosing a solid and implying the solid form. The third drawing has been taken a stage further: the addition of tone and a cast shadow make the object appear real and tactile.

Try a still-life subject, using as little tone as possible—suggesting the form with your lines. The line here is given meaning because I looked at the surface of the fruit rather than at the outline.

To make a linear drawing of a solid object, you must look for planes such as those shown in the bottom picture.

19

Tone and colour

Tone can be used to represent colour, as in the drawing here. The girl's dark hair and sweater, the colour of the cheques on her jacket and patterns on her skirt are all represented by different tones of grey.

The drawing opposite, on the other hand, is not concerned with colour of clothes or skin; the areas of light and dark represent the fall of light and shadow on the sitter.

It is important to distinguish between tone used to represent colour, and tone used to suggest planes.

In the picture opposite, the side of the girl's nose is dark and the front light, but the colour of side and front is the same. Tone has been used to show the planes which make the form of the nose. I could have described the form of the blazer in the same way, but to do so would have made the drawing fussy, and the form of the face is more important to the picture than that of the blazer. The blazer's form is therefore *implied*, rather than *described*. Always draw with purpose. Each part of a picture must support the design as a whole as well as representing the appearance of the subject.

Be similarly selective when using tone to indicate colour. The shape and colour of hair or different garments can be as central to a drawing as the representation of solid forms. But look for an overall pattern and pay careful attention to it as your drawing proceeds. Pay attention also to the light areas among these colour shapes, which provide their own pattern. The paper on which your drawing is made sets the tonal 'key': light areas (even if they are far from white) are represented by the white paper in this drawing. All dark areas are relative to this whiteness; if you make them too black you may flatten the area rather than giving it an impression of form and reality.

Studies
in tone

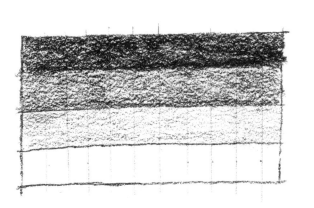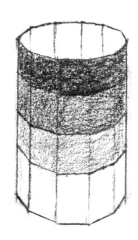

Divide a piece of drawing paper into several bands. Make the top band black and leave the bottom one white. Darken the middle bands in progressive stages from black to white by painting them with different mixtures of black and white poster paints. Then fold the paper into vertical strips and stick the ends together to make a faceted cylinder as in the diagram. Stand the cylinder on a table in a side light and observe how each plane changes in relation to the direction of the light. Big changes occur in the white band; comparatively small ones in the black.

Next, make drawings of still-life objects which include your faceted tone scale. The more you practise on inanimate objects, the better equipped you will be when you come to draw children. A still-life doesn't move; whereas a young child rarely stays completely still for more

than a few minutes (twenty if you are very lucky). Drawing still life will teach you to understand form at your own pace, and the form of a child's head is not basically different from that of a fruit.

25

The head

You will learn a lot from making several quick drawings of the same head. Get your sitter to turn away from you, drawing by drawing, until the nose has disappeared from your angle of vision.

Notice, in the drawings opposite, how foreshortened the nose is when the head is tilted back—the tip of it being brought very close to the eye.

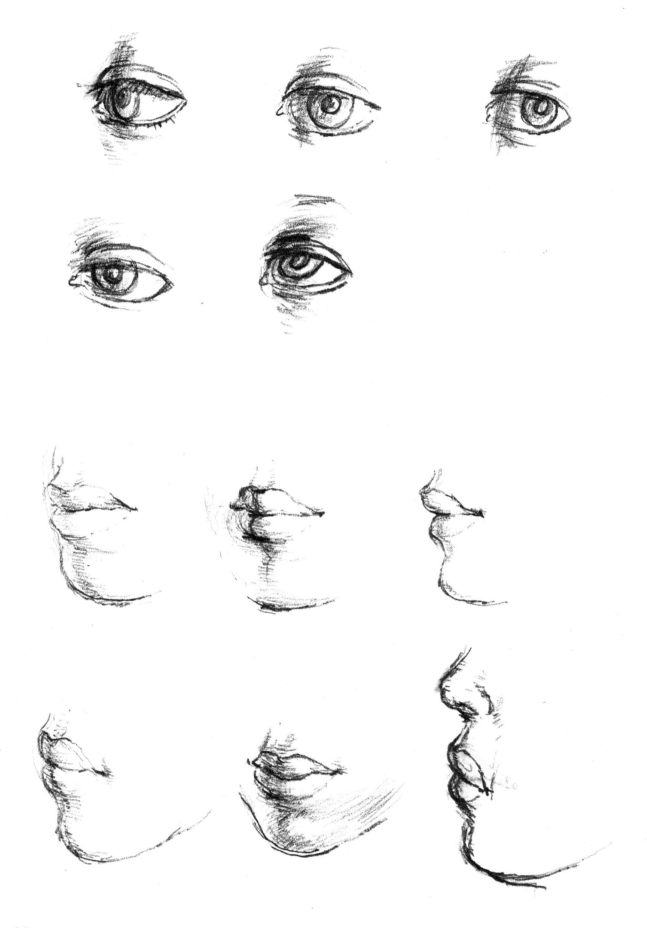

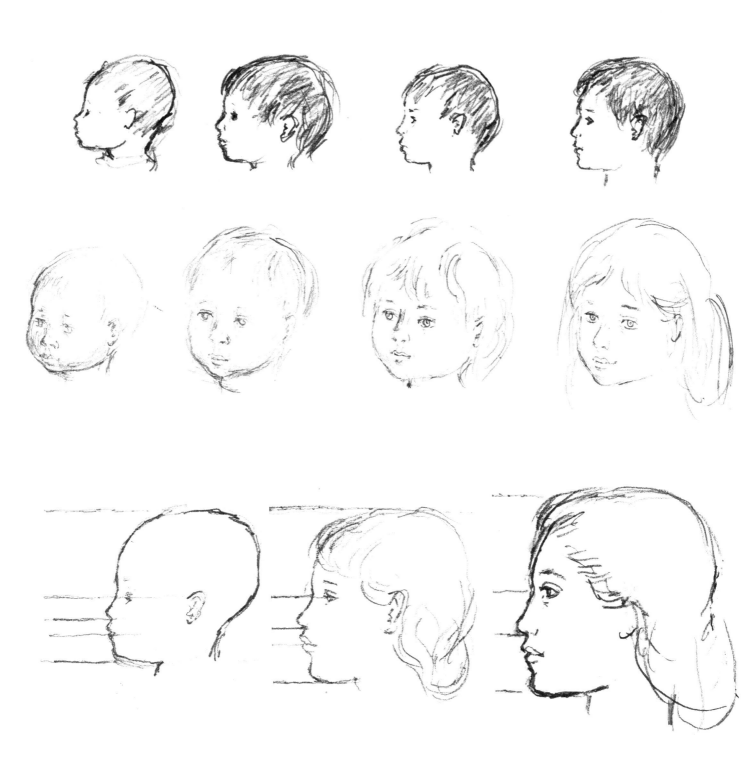

Draw eyes and mouths in several positions also—as in the sketches left—practising the tonal skills you learned from drawing still life.

Above: the two upper sets of drawings show the characteristic development of the head in the first ten years of a child's life. The lower set shows the characteristic head proportions of a baby, a ten-year-old and an adult.

Pen and wash

For a pen-and-wash drawing it is particularly important to have a subject who will sit still. Put him or her in a strong side light if you are a beginner, because it is easier then to understand the effects of light and shade. The tonal studies suggested on pages 24-5 are good experience for pen and wash, as for pencil and other media.

Use black waterproof ink and a paper that will absorb the wash readily; a non-absorbent paper tends to produce uncontrollable puddles. Use the pen for lines and the wash for areas. Don't try to 'model' with the wash; concentrate on where to put it rather than producing varieties of tone. If you understand the solid shape you are representing (pages 24-5), you will place the tone where it makes the form rather than copying the appearance of the subject.

First draw with the pen; then help the form you are making with the wash. Mix the wash as you need it in small quantities; a white saucer will show how dark it is. With the right paper, you will be able to work over the first wash after a few minutes. The incomplete head on the left indicates the procedure. For your first drawings in pen and wash, look for the pattern in the subject as a single dark tone against the light areas.

A baby

A subject as mobile as a six-month-old baby needs skill and directness of drawing. You may have to make many new starts, and will probably have several drawings on the go at once, on the same piece of paper. Get someone to hold the baby's attention in some way. Draw an eye and hope that he will resume the same position later so that you can draw the other one. Gradually, you will learn what the baby looks like and see your way to a complete drawing. In the final drawing (page 34) washes of colour were added and unnecessary lines taken out with process white.

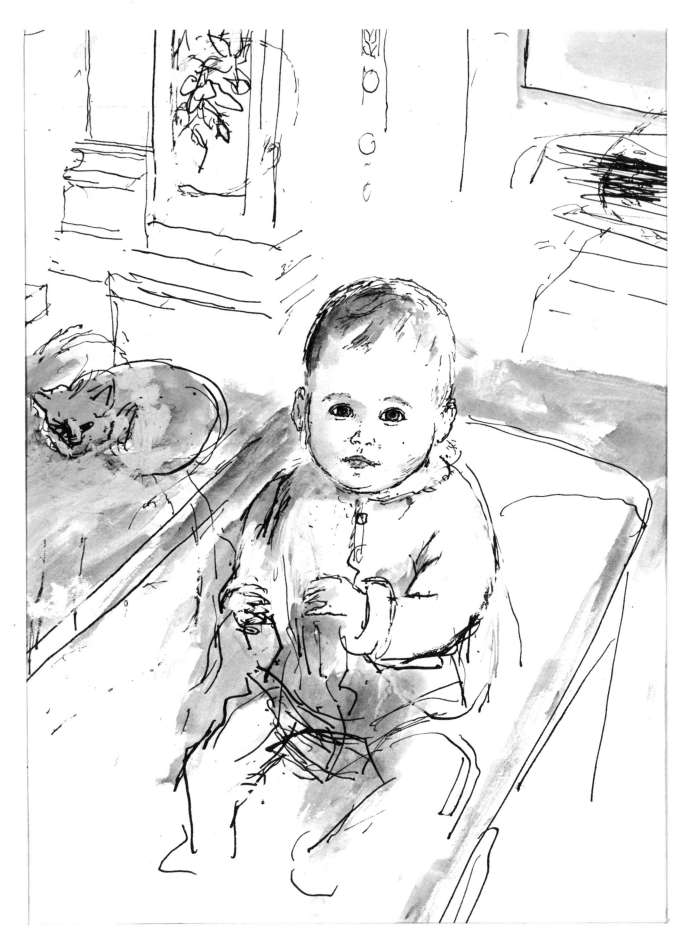

A twelve-year-old

In contrast, the subject of this drawing was pleased to pose with squash racquet in his favourite outfit and controlled enough to sit still for half an hour or more. The younger child joined in voluntarily, dressed to suit.

Young children

When young children come especially to pose, you must start instantly. They are keyed up for the occasion, but their interest and co-operation will last only a limited time. Each of these children posed for about twenty minutes. The 'extra' from page 34 turned up again for the left-hand drawing.

Make the most of a
uniform, putting in the
various badges, etc., and
represent the colour where
you can. The child has not
dressed up for you to study
nuances of light and
shade.

Older children

If your sitter is an older child, let her walk about and talk while you are getting ready to draw. She will be more at ease when she poses, and you will have had the opportunity to observe such physical characteristics as the shape of her head and such personal traits of stance and movement as how she holds her hands. Choose a pose which will display these characteristics and keep them in mind; it is easy to forget them when you are paying attention to such details as getting the corner of the lips right or the eye.

The two drawings on the left were in a sense trials. In the first, the dress was too casual and the model looked too old; the second is too heavy and the exuberance of hair is missing.

If the sitter is to remain awake she must understand that, within reason, she can move when she likes. Once the pose is established, she can return to it quite easily.

At the age of fourteen, a co-operative sitter will stay still for quite a long time. This one chose her own clothes for the occasion, and her dark skin looked good against the light cream blouse. Her shoes and general grooming had a sophistication and individuality about them which required an elegant chair.

The drawing started like the one on this page: the eyes first, then the nose, cheek, lips, the hair indicated, the collar and tie. A measurement located the hands. As the drawing proceeded door-wards it was necessary to note the perspective, as shown in the lower drawing here.

The background to the figure was drawn in last. It is preferable, although not always possible, to have the figure there when you draw the background—even if she doesn't hold her pose—so that you can see the scale and relationship between them.

Children in movement

Here, the 'extra' from pages 35-6 came into his own.

You can only learn how to draw by drawing. Practise as often as possible, attempting to draw children whatever they are doing. You may never start if you wait for them to stay still. With young children, rapid drawing is essential. There is no time to model the form; you must imply it with line. The child on this page thought he was keeping the same pose while I made these three drawings.

Don't leave out the accessories; they are often related to the action and the pose, and help to explain both. If a pose is expressed in the fingertips, draw them first.

Dancing class

Dancing is a subject that tempts many artists and students, in spite of its difficulties. Children in a dancing class have particular charm. The artist's double challenge is to convey the rhythm of figures moving in unison, and at the same time the individuality of each child. The figures are rarely still, but movements are repeated many times; it is necessary to draw very much from memory.

Start by drawing one figure fairly carefully, rather than rushing after several almost disassociated figures. Then (since your drawing is of a room with figures in it) sketch in the space of the room. Wherever figures appear in the room, try to draw them quickly in this place in the picture, concentrating on size and perspective. In more detail, draw the dancing mistress, the pianist and the children when they rest. Pay attention to the room itself. Its height, space and decoration help to set the scene and give scale and meaning to the figures. And, even if your drawings of the children are slight, you will end with a picture which has space and movement and in which you have attempted all that the subject offers.

48